11-13

BEING FRANK WITH ANNE

A Poetic Tribute to Anne Frank

Phyllis C. Johnson

PUBLISHED BY WORDS AT PLAY PUBLISHING

Published by Words at Play Publishing
PO Box 9643
Chesapeake, VA 23321
© 2008 by Community Press, 1st Edition
© 2011 by Phyllis Johnson, 2nd Edition
Cover design—Book Graphics
Layout—Savannah Frierson, SJF Books
Author photo—Bonnie Munden

Library of Congress Control Number 2007939232

ISBN-10: 1467951439
ISBN-13: 978-1467951432

Printed in the United States of America

Visit the website at www.beingfrankwithanne.com

REVIEWS

"With gratitude and personal regards." (Note accompanying signature in a copy of *Being Frank with Anne*)

- Miep Gies (just before her passing at age 100)

"I have read many books about Anne, but this day-to-day comment in poetry and its many facets is interesting and moving. I am sure Anne would like it very much."
— Buddy Elias, Anne Frank's first cousin writing as CEO of Anne Frank Fonds in Basel

"Reading the poems in *Being Frank with Anne* took me back to when I was a young girl reading the diary."
- Natasha Trethewey—2007 Pulitzer Prize Winner for Poetry

"I carefully read *Being Frank with Anne*. What an inspiring book, one which I feel certain Anne would appreciate."
- Carolyn Kreiter-Foronda, 2007-2008 Virginia's Poet Laureate

DEDICATION

This is in memory of my dear friend, Krystyna Bublick, former chairman of the Holocaust Commission of the United Jewish Federation of Tidewater and daughter of Adela Lach Piasecki, a Holocaust survivor who was also at Bergen Belsen. I also dedicate it to my family and friends who have supported me during my writing career and the many hours spent at the computer.

PROLOGUE

With a heart and soul that was mature beyond her years, Anne Frank has inspired and encouraged millions. Her diary haunted me as a young girl and has spoken to me for years. Written before Erin Gruell inspired the Freedom Writers with the diary, I penned this unrhymed poetic interpretation of the diary entries over the course of a summer. I spoke with Erin before publishing this book and she seemed excited about my writing it.

The first edition of this book has taken an interesting journey. It has been archived at the Anne Frank House in Amsterdam and posted on the New York Anne Frank Center website bookstore under commentary. I was humbled to have had it reviewed by her first cousin, Buddy Elias, CEO of the Anne Frank Fonds in Basel. It was also a huge thrill when Miep Gies (the woman who helped hide the Frank family) heard of the book and asked for copies. She returned one copy from the Netherlands with her signature in it and a sweet note. This all happened during the year before she passed away at age 100.

When reading Being Frank with Anne, you'll see that the dates of the entries inspiring each poem are for cross referencing with the diary entries. Analyzing each entry took me on an emotional journey. Noting Anne's changes in mood and the moods of those around her, I followed the passages of time in the Secret Annexe.

In chronological order in a world not logical, days turned into weeks, weeks turned into months, and months became years. Some images stayed with me and spoke to me more than others but the experience of interpreting her life in this way was powerful. Let your heart and mind carry you into her life and thoughts as seen through these poetic images in this book.

Sunday, June 14, 1942

Birthday gifts
chocolates, a puzzle, a broach
the greatest of all- a diary
Days to come,
your life is a semi-sweet puzzle.
Your diary books your passage to sanity.
A plaid lifeguard.

MONDAY, JUNE 15, 1942

Thoughts included friends,
a movie called "The Lighthouse Keeper"
with Rin Tin Tin.
Lighthouses, a source of light and direction
worth barking about.
Your own quiet strength
to surge forth as a beacon
with no barking but carefully murmured
whispers.

SATURDAY, JUNE 20, 1942

Patient paper
point well taken
as words join hands and
lie flat on paper.
Paper lies patiently,
not moving, not arching eyebrows
or impatient hand gestures
to speed a conversation.

"Kitty" you called it.
Like investing funds in a kitty,
you invested your inner guts and soul.
Your dark haired roots
of family tree crowned
with yellow stars
stood strong in spite of
poisoned soil all around.

SATURDAY, JUNE 20, 1942

An ice cream Oasis
like ping pong balls atop a cone,
you raised a racket
among buddies.
Sweat dripped fast as ice cream.

Bike spokes spun round
spoken words from hopeful beaus
either returned by your racket
or ignored,
out of court,
out of mind.

SUNDAY, JUNE 21, 1942

Hedging bets,
pruned and sheered by odds.
Worried eyebrows knitting sweaters,
pass or fail and who?
Nine teachers doing balancing acts,
juggling grades,
silencing students, including you—
Chatterbox.
Same name.
You, a forced report,
a failed goal by
math master
for your mouth
rambled on...
like a babbling brook.
"Quack, quack, quack."

The new assigned paper,
one you couldn't duck,
ghostwritten in rhyme
enjoyed by all.
Freedom to speak
words, spontaneous verbiage
gushing among sitting ducks.

WEDNESDAY, JUNE 24, 1942

The dentist drilled teeth,
the government drilled rules.
Trams, a forbidden luxury,
aware of a stolen bike,
you had long walks and a long face.
Longing always for new friends,
then, a new face
handsome and sixteen,
wanted to come along.
You said "Yes."
Who needs trams anyway?

TUESDAY, JUNE 30, 1942

Gentle and quiet,
a tranquilizer
she was.
Fanny– your competition
but Harry found you more
exciting.
He found Zionists
his rebellion.
Etched in your memory
as were other boys.
A fickle pickle of sorts.

FRIDAY, JULY 3, 1942

Fickle faded.
Shades of love and
sweet eats.
Like hot cross buns,
a hot cross Daddy.
Out too late,
curfewed too soon.
Ten minutes
more or less.
Less time,
more freedom,
a soul confides
you're the one.
Fitting remark
following the
parental intro.
Love shaded by
blinders of youth,
sweet biscuits
and sweet times.

SUNDAY, JULY 5, 1942

Evidence of skill—
family grades.
Parents were A+,
life given a good score
and your outlook positive
though anxious.
Hushed words of hiding,
hidden words
though meaning revealed.
Visions of good days
frozen in mental freeze frames.
Hopes that clocks would
stop with happy faces.

WEDNESDAY, JULY 8, 1942

Pounding heart,
a pound on the door.
A call-up.
Who?
Daddy?
Mummy?
Margot? No.
This can't be.
Plans fall into place
like the outer
rim of a puzzle.
The inner rim of family
contrasts the center.
Interlocking,
entwined
layered with clothes
and strength.
You slipped away
Goodbye, Moortje.

THURSDAY, JULY 9, 1942

Yellow stars
in heavy rain.
Shades of joy
and a secret passage
to a new life.
Plain grey door
to a plain grey life.
Colored by hope
that the Secret Annexe
wouldn't be forever.

FRIDAY, JULY 10, 1942

Many boxes
cardboard and empty
scattered like
wagons around
a campfire.
Smoke in the form of
fatigue and sweat
took Mummy and Margot.
Daddy and you,
keepers of the lighthouse.

Next day
organization
then
REALIZATION.

SATURDAY, JULY 11, 1942

Chiming clock,
faithful,
reassuring,
reminds you
you're not invisible.
Celebrity collage
applied by paste
serves to glue your
sanity in place.
Burnt peas in
anxiety soup.
Strips for curtains
and stripes for sunlight.
Oppression and
no coughs,
no exits in sight.

FRIDAY, AUGUST 14, 1942

Van Daan's
came
and Peter is shy.
The folding tea table
they brought
held stories of the
house they left behind
and a lot of disappearances.
Rumors
flew like
swallows in the wind.
Wind that you longed to feel
as you
sat at the tea table.

FRIDAY, AUGUST 21, 1942

Cupboard bare except for
souls inside.
The plan that
really knocked you out

Reminders of
the way in
or out
but not really.

A dull Peter,
as hard to like
as the wood he hammers.

WEDNESDAY, SEPTEMBER 2, 1942

Wasted breath and
heated words
like an oven flows.
Hypochondria runs rampant
like a diseased mind.
Peter-
as stingy with optimism
as Mrs. Van Daan
is with sheets.
The forbidden book
Peter sat reading as you
read between the lines.
Forbidden as the outside.
Attic reading,
thousands of words.
Pieces of
broken china
and broken spirits,
fragments of reality.

MONDAY, SEPTEMBER 21, 1942

Food scraps
and scrapping folks.
Daddy's family tree is sprouting new branches
and leaves.
Leaves turn in
pages of your
books and papers
of your mind.

FRIDAY, SEPTEMBER 25, 1942

Lemonade and
moth biscuits,
cheek stroking by Peter.
Why can't he
fly away with moths?
Only way out—
through an envelope.
Licking envelopes,
but not your problem.

SUNDAY, SEPTEMBER 27, 1942

A green Mrs. Van Daan
blushes red and
you don't.
Green as the vegetables
she pushes on you.
Barbed words abound as the
invisible barbed
fence between your
family and hers.
One day you'll climb
that fence.

Monday, September 28, 1942

Fertilized complaints
about you reap huge harvests.
Explosion inevitable.
Showdown with
Mummy and Mrs. Van Daan
Left fallout
to be swept out
with a broom.

SUNDAY, SEPTEMBER 29, 1942

A washtub
in private places
for soaping private parts.
A plumber's visit,
no moving,
no whispers.
Three days
of a glass jar.
Jarring your nerves and seeing
as clear as glass
that silence is torture.

THURSDAY, OCTOBER 1, 1942

Mrs. Van Daan's
birthday carnations
as red as her actions
around Pim.
Face stroking
fire stoking
unrequited love,
much to your delight.
Funny, witty, surprising.
Peter decides to
skirt the issue of boredom
and wear one.
Trading places,
amusement.

SATURDAY, OCTOBER 3, 1942

Mummy had a row
and you needed a boat.
Rocky waves
and rough waters.
Daddy is a lifejacket
and your studies are the straps.

FRIDAY, OCTOBER 9, 1942

Donuts go by the dozen,
so have your Jewish friends
by way of Gestapo.
Cattle truck
but not cattle.
Shaved heads—
but not men.

FRIDAY, OCTOBER 16, 1942

You did shorthand
and long math
then traded secrets,
Margot and you.
Like blossoms on
an apple tree,
your affection for
Peter ripens slowly.
You offer
him an apple
and wait for results.

TUESDAY, OCTOBER 20, 1942

Panic strikes
as a carpenter
on the outside
rattles your insides.

Is he opening
the cupboard door?
Fear grabs you
like a coiled snake.
A familiar voice
calls out and is
invited in—
Mr. Koophius.

Your heart hammers
out a rhythmic
thank you for
not being
discovered
one more time.

THURSDAY, OCTOBER 29, 1942

Pim and a high fever—
as hot as Mrs. Van Daan
if she knew about
the possessions left behind
or the removal of.
Unknown loss of lovely china and chairs
as she sits in earnest
and chews anxiety for breakfast.

As you read, "Eva's Youth"
your own goes by
like a candle under a cover.
It glows invisible but hot.

A prayer book in German
serves as a fan for spiritual fire
just as the chimney will
draw fire for you tomorrow.

Fever and fire...

SATURDAY, NOVEMBER 7, 1942

Envy of Margot's
treatment
grows like a green
fungus
invading your
emotions
slowly like
a creeping fog.
Dimly, you see
Mummy's
criticism and
as if under a bright
light any harsh
words
from Daddy arise and
linger—
a rebuking beacon.

Being good without
example,
getting along while
being opposite,
or at least trying.
Torn while being
treated
as two people—
the sensible and the
silly.

Confusion reigns as
an inner struggle for
independence and
love
boils below the
surface.

A seething cauldron.

Monday, November 9, 1942

Peter
sweet and sixteen,
gets Monopoly to play
and a monopoly
on your time.

Optimism reigns as
Britain's defending
and hopes go up.

Beans come down,
a seam splits and
a thunderstorm of
beans surround your
feet like sand on
a beach.

Waves of laughter wash
over Peter and you.
Laughter,
purifying
and wonderful.

TUESDAY, NOVEMBER 10, 1942

Seven—
a lucky number
for seven hidden souls.
Then eight,
enlarging the family and broadening the inner
circle.
Mr. Dussel—
a dentist,
one who maintains teeth so one can chew.
Just as you must
maintain hope
so you can survive
in this Secret Annexe,
the family of souls united
in fear and love.

THURSDAY, NOVEMBER 12, 1942

Dentist Dussel settling business
before settling in
the Secret Annexe.

Trying to tie up loose
ends with knots,
knots in your stomachs
as he hesitates
to move for several
days of waiting.
Patients to see for him—
no patience for you.

TUESDAY, NOVEMBER 17, 1942

Arriving twenty past eleven
Dussel is shocked
shocked by who awaits him
and the obscurity
now, seeing past the
intentional lies- he
derives at a purpose.

THURSDAY, NOVEMBER 19, 1942

Shared quarters
with Dussel—
a nice man
but full of questions.
Drilling on hiding,
giving info on friends
in trouble.
Unlucky friends,
marching into death
unless freed
for a price
on their heads.
Your own freedom
pays a price of
guilt,
sorrow for those
less fortunate.
Your sympathy is snuggled
in a warm blanket.
A quilt of guilt.

FRIDAY, NOVEMBER 20, 1942

Laughter
struggles to escape
worried lips as
eyes that cry tears
try to twinkle and
laugh,
a certain solitude settles in
amidst memories
of former friendships.
A bright countenance
upon a grey background
struggles to maintain
position as you
juggle today with
yesterday in that
on again, off again
world of emotions.

Saturday, November 28, 1942

Framed fascination,
lifestyles under glass
under scrutiny,
yours.
Having meals, cleaning teeth,
making home movies,
theirs.
Feeling like fuzz,
being picked on.

Monday, December 7, 1942

A ten minute flame,
candles and Chanukah.

An eight o'clock surprise,
presents and St. Nicholas.

A simple delight,
a doll and a poem—

Celebration.

THURSDAY, DECEMBER 10, 1942

Encased like the
sausages you watched being made,
minced with mingled
laughter and anxiety,
poured into a spout
of opportunity and
funneled into a
casing of discretion.
Hung like drying meat
for the duration,
you saw bad teeth and a
bad attitude—
Dussel
works on Mrs. Van Daan
and laughter flows like
a spit fountain,
splitting the seams of your
casings.

SUNDAY, DECEMBER 13, 1942

Slit sighted
curtain watching,
you see dirty children
pass by–
just like your life.

A noisy dog
announces his presence
and your quiet presence
in hiding makes
your insides
howl in sympathy
for the grim Jews outside.

Rain begins to fall
and umbrellas
with legs come
into view.
Rain
tries to wash away
the misery outside
but falls short.

TUESDAY, DECEMBER 22, 1942

Extra butter has
greased your gears and
compliments abound
for Mrs. Van Daan,
who with bruised ribs and spirit
reveals her former cheer and
tidiness to be a
missed gift.

WEDNESDAY, JANUARY 13, 1943

Like old rags,
families are torn apart,
ragged shreds of dignity.
Fibers exposed,
revealing raw nerves.

The cold and hungry
run about with
hollow eyes that
scream in the night.

SATURDAY, JANUARY 30, 1943

Mummy draws the bow
and releases her arrows
of criticism at you,
as do all the others.
Tired of being a bull's eye,
you wish to close yours
and blink it away.
To become someone else,
not criticized,
not ridiculed.

FRIDAY, FEBRUARY 5, 1943

An example
you are not...
at least you are told.
Margot and Peter,
looking old and boring
lurk in contrast
to your youth
and mealtime
is as strained as
baby food.

SATURDAY, FEBRUARY 27, 1943

A card index
for books.
A memory index
for life on the outside.
Now inside,
in a house just sold,
your secret threatened
like your share of butter.
The future is not as
sweet and smooth as the
rationed butter you crave
on your plate.

WEDNESDAY, MARCH 10, 1943

Guns pounding
like your heartbeat.
Candle flames burn
like hope in the dark—
when Pim allows it.
Rumbling in the attic
is rampant
like the jumbled throbbing
thoughts through
your mind.
Mouschi goes after
the cats in the attic
just as Pim
chases after fears
hanging over your head.

FRIDAY, MARCH 12, 1943

Fish for felines
and beans for you,
more than you care to eat.
You wish to swim away,
swim like the former life of
Mouschi's dinner.
Nearly shoeless—
newly a barber,
your sheared wardrobe of shoes
dreadfully cut
like a bad hairdo.

FRIDAY, MARCH 19, 1943

Traps for black money abound,
ready to spring
and catch the hidden,
unlucky foxes
licking their wounds
like the soldiers
greeting the Führer.

THURSDAY, MARCH 25, 1943

Noise on the outside
causes panic on the inside.
Rumbling tummies
keep you stirred up.
A quiet clock disturbs your security
and a winkless night
beams moonlight
over the Secret Annexe.

SATURDAY, MARCH 27, 1943

Studies absorb your thoughts and
mythology is big.
If only your lifestyle
was a myth.

It would be setting fires to fears,
if you awoke to
find it all a dream.

Then the stories of
dirty slaughterhouses could all
go up in smoke,
just as the Labor Exchange has.

THURSDAY, APRIL 1, 1943

Illness abounds
and Pim has a real need to
hear talking below.
Conferences.
You drop not so easily
to eavesdrop,
ear pressed to floor.
Long talks start
to bore you
until sleep creeps in
and resides.
Information is
soon forgotten.

FRIDAY, APRIL 2, 1943

Your mother's apron strings
were never there,
at least you didn't
see them.

Now she dangles
a thread at you
and you push it away,
believing it not
really attached to the apron.

You find it hard
having no children of
your own
to see past her faults
yet now recognize them
in yourself.

Recognition
but rejection.

TUESDAY, APRIL 27, 1943

Reality is a war zone
on the inside
while air raids are prevalent
on the outside.
Planes circle in the dark
as do the rings around your eyes.
Dry bread and flat coffee,
spuds and spinach
are table fare for you and
your comrades.

SATURDAY, MAY 1, 1943

There are as many holes
in manners
as there are in dishcloths
and spanking clean is a
thing of the past.

Corsets are too tight for holding
bras too small for breathing,
a ragged state of affairs.

A timid suitcase
packed with your things,
but where to?

TUESDAY, MAY 18, 1943

Four parachutists jump
from the frying pan
into the fire.

A red glow shines
announcing a deafening
round of guns,
that thunder through
your house,
disturbing rest
that never was.

SUNDAY, JUNE 13, 1943

Like a rose among thorns,
this day is a jewel.
A poem penned in love
is presented by Pim
and your favorite things
distract you from your
least favorable situation.

Temporary sanity being
the best gift of all.

TUESDAY, JUNE 15, 1943

Vossen's illness
will separate you
from the outer world
like a vault,
the combination of
which, no one will ever
know.

A big radio will be
traded in- replaced
by a black baby set
whose clandestine songs will
cheer you as much.

SUNDAY, JULY 11, 1943

Living your life
through books and radio,
you are carried away to
other worlds.
Away from confinement,
away from rations,
away from criticism.
Piped in music
is a pipeline pumping power to your soul,
helping you to see life richer,
in a brighter way—
despite your eyes,
which are getting poor.

TUESDAY, JULY 13, 1943

Fights with Dussel over a table
of four legs,
leaves you without
a leg to stand on.
Your learning's treated
as unimportant fluff.
Your "fluff"
defended by Pim
is given a backbone
and you get to reclaim
those four legs.

FRIDAY, JULY 16, 1943

Forced openings and crowbars,
missing cashboxes and checks
and not so sweet
stolen sugar coupons
rattle you, the occupants
of the Secret Annexe.

Thievery makes you insecure,
but it's only things.
The security of your souls
lies foremost in your minds
and strength must become a
noble fortress.

MONDAY, JULY 19, 1943

A morbid mosaic
of grey ruins,
red gunfire
and pale white faces
of orphaned children
interlock into pieces of
a nightmarish puzzle,
having no borders,
no logic.

FRIDAY, JULY 23, 1943

Thoughts of the outside
conjure up a
bubbling pot of wishes.
This steaming cauldron
reeks of cakes and coffee,
hot soaks and cinema,
schooling and seeing loved ones.

MONDAY, JULY 26, 1943

Sirens and bombing
break the silence
but the small voice
of fear inside you
speaks louder.
Everyone is on the lookout
and prospects of the future as
unclear as the vision
through the rising smoke outside.
Mussolini resigned—
there is light at the end of the
tunnel.

THURSDAY, JULY 29, 1943

Finding dull
a book recommended
by Dussel.
You mention it
and in contrast,
to its dullness,
receive a sharp reprimand.
Complaints
about Mrs. Van Daan
stretch out as
much as the
day is long.

TUESDAY, AUGUST 3, 1943

You itch for
freedom amidst
fleas,
teeth clenching,
tear jerking air raids.

WEDNESDAY, AUGUST 4, 1943

Nightly duties;
bed fixing,
moustache bleaching,
body washing,
snore listening.

Recording a night
in the life of
the confined,
an attempt to
be normal
in an abnormal world.
A flurry of hair curling
and manicures,
as if it really
mattered.

THURSDAY, AUGUST 5, 1943

Like spokes
on a wheel,
you all sit
around a radio
plugged in to
get news of the
outside.

Quarter to two,
everyone sleeps
but you.
Sitting at the
writing table,
you feel your very soul
come alive.

Monday, August 9, 1943

You describe
members in the Annexe.
A kind of hodge podge
vegetable soup.
Each having his
or her own
colors and tastes.
Each complementing
or contrasting
the other. They form
a blend in this
sink or swim
lifestyle.
Each bobbing for
air and attention,
a fair share...
Some stirrers,
some settlers,
some sinkers.

TUESDAY, AUGUST 10, 1943

Fancy footwear
and forbidden books.
Shoes that make
you look taller
and a book that makes
Hitler look smaller.

WEDNESDAY, AUGUST 18, 1943

Peeling potatoes
brings out
discussion on the
best way to peel.

Strong opinions
peel away confidence.
A constant
Self-examination
maintained,
internal cleansing,
and constant
self-improvement.

FRIDAY, AUGUST 20, 1943

Everyone has
his or her own job,
even the cats.
Like well oiled
machinery,
the whole must
work together
when possible
in order to survive.

MONDAY, AUGUST 23, 1943

You eat silence and slop
for breakfast and
reading wrinkles
announce Pim's activity.
Three taps
reveal
three meals.
The first of which
being breakfast.

Friday, September 10, 1943

Mr. Koophius
helps you
stomach the situation,
now his must
be worked on.

THURSDAY, SEPTEMBER 16, 1943

Relations
strain like cheesecloth
and the warehouseman
is suspicious.
Everyone's face
is as long
as the winter
that looms ahead.

WEDNESDAY, SEPTEMBER 29, 1943

Nerves unravel
as shopping lists
never stop rolling.
A steady flow
of needs
keeps you too busy
to think as
clouds of
disagreement hover.
When will it rain?

SUNDAY, OCTOBER 17, 1943

Pim has a quilt
of diplomacy,
always patching
things up.
Koophius is
selling threads
for the Van Daan's.
Needles of nerves but
no one in stitches.

FRIDAY, OCTOBER 29, 1943

Warmth in the
form of animal fur
caused a lack of
warmth between
the Van Daans.

Your fear has
more wings than the
desired birds outside
that don't
come and sing anymore.

MONDAY, NOVEMBER 8, 1943

Fear resides on the range
and coward rides
tall in the saddle.
Feet in stirrups,
you hang on for the ride.

Ominous clouds
overhead,
closing in,
suffocating—
light and air
diminishing.

THURSDAY, NOVEMBER 11, 1943

Your favorite pen
met its fate—
accidental cremation.
Swept up with
beans and tossed,
the pen that had
been through many words—
words that didn't
have to be eaten
like beans.

WEDNESDAY, NOVEMBER 17, 1943

Illness invites
longing for
someone's company.
Elli's.
Illness invites
longing for nicer food—
it's milk and porridge
for Koophius.
Illness of anger invites
silence between
Annexe members,
love and gratitude invite
a much nicer atmosphere
in which to live.

Saturday, November 27, 1943

Big sad eyes
haunt you.
Eyes of Lies,
your friend,
who beyond your
help is surely
suffering a life you
only imagine.
Guilt and concern
wash over you in
steady waves.
As you sink
into the sand- a
heart's cry goes,
comfort for her
in her need.

Monday, December 6, 1943

Taking steps to
a merry holiday—
you and Pim pen poems
to place in objects
one steps into—
shoes.
Coupled with
small gifts these
verses help reverse
feelings that
take everyone a step
backward.
Diplomacy
wrapped in a bow.

WEDNESDAY, DECEMBER 22, 1943

Harmony has built
strong branches in
the tree.
Nestled in the
branches are
gifts of love.
Sprouting
green growths over
the holidays,
showing
promise of cooperation
for members of the Annexe.

FRIDAY, DECEMBER 24, 1943

Invisible hands reach
out from your heart
and wish to grab
fun that flourishes
on the outside.
To laugh,
to run,
to breathe fresh air.
What a dream it would be.
Oh strong one,
with your proud head
held high—
letting only Kitty know
what's on your mind.
Fun.

SATURDAY, DECEMBER 25, 1943

With growing,
comes understanding,
with understanding
comes a real knowing.
Knowing the inside of Pim.
The inside that
stays hidden to
those who don't
look deeply into
his heart.

MONDAY, DECEMBER 27, 1943

For the holiday,
a cake of peace
from which slices
you ate.
If only you could
pass pieces
around the world.
Love for the batter
and hope for the icing.

WEDNESDAY, DECEMBER 29, 1943

Your thoughts go
back to Granny
and her
aloneness despite
the love
she knew existed
loomed like a shadow
and shadows of your friend,
Lies, flit through your mind.
Prayers grow wings and fly
upward.
You fight fear with
a dull sword of faith.

SUNDAY, JANUARY 2, 1944

Like a review,
you study Kitty
and come face to face
with an old you.

With clenched teeth and fists
and anger that seethes.
Now that mirror changes and
the glass is clear
and you see the other side
as well as your own.

WEDNESDAY, JANUARY 5, 1944

Needing her for a
mother instead of a friend,
Mummy.
Needing security
instead of embarrassment
maturing.

Needing a friend
instead of isolation.
Anne.

Thursday, January 6, 1944

You and Peter
work on crosswords
but exchange none.
Sinking into blue eyes,
you try to see behind them.
Dark eyes in your dreams
look back into yours.
Dreams of desire
and dreams of Grandma
float through your mind,
fleeting and velvet.

FRIDAY, JANUARY 7, 1944

Memories of old
beaus wrap around
your heart like a ribbon.
Wrapped the tightest
are thoughts of Peter Wessel.
The ends curl
around in your subconscious
like a corkscrew,
opening a bottle
of longing to see his face.

WEDNESDAY, JANUARY 12, 1944

A homemade dance frock
with bow at center
takes center stage in your desires.
Supple and limber
you become
as flexible as
Margot's attitude
toward you.
You examine
your own role in
relationships,
sometimes the rose,
sometimes the weed.

SATURDAY, JANUARY 15, 1944

Fights over rations
drown out rumbling tummies
and there is sourness
over Mummy's birthday sugar.
Jealousy reared green
and ugly
and your disappointment
over selfishness
grows like ivy
on a trellis.

SATURDAY, JANUARY 22, 1944

You mentally
multiply redeeming
factors,
giving Annexe
members a
product of second chance.

MONDAY, JANUARY 24, 1944

Facts of life
being important
Tom or Thomasina?
Peter,
wise and right
shows Boche's
true colors.

THURSDAY, JANUARY 27, 1944

Your mental map of marvels
includes stellar photos
and family trees—
Branches, twigs, a brush
against the past.

FRIDAY, JANUARY 28, 1944

Stories and jokes
grow stale as bread
and you wish to make
bread pudding of it all.
Gratitude for your
helpers rises like yeast
and warms you like
a cooked loaf.

THURSDAY, FEBRUARY 3, 1944

Flood warnings
pour like tidal waves
bringing ebb tides
of emotion.

Taking stock of stock
and discussions
of your fates
consume the day.
You surrender anxiety
to the wind,
ready to blow when
the wind blows.

SATURDAY, FEBRUARY 12, 1944

Longing to absorb
the world outside
through a crack in the window.
A window in your soul
dares to raise the
blinds and become
totally open.
Open, fresh and new.

Sunday, February 13, 1944

You notice someone
noticing you,
Peter.
It gives you a
nice feeling,
Joy.
you want something
you don't get...
solitude.

MONDAY, FEBRUARY 14, 1944

Fellowship found in
the form of
compared notes.
You and Peter,
frustration and fits.
Misunderstood
and needing
to confide in
willing ears.
Amusement at having
connected
like a chain
of paper clips,
you against them,
those who don't understand,
not like Peter.

WEDNESDAY, FEBRUARY 16, 1944

Margot's birthday
and you get a gift of
Peter's conversation.
Picking potatoes for
peeling and
peeling away
layers of
loneliness, revealing
his insecurity and a
hint of dishonesty
about which you appreciate his
ultimate honesty.

Friday, February 18, 1944

A special meaning
for your life,
Peter.
A special feeling
in your life,
fondness.
Talking takes on
a whole new
meaning
and rivals,
sweet rivals
are none.

SATURDAY, FEBRUARY 19, 1944

The sands of time
today stretched out
like a deserted beach
and your tears joined
hands and washed waves
over your long face.
Was your friendship
with Peter real or
imagined?
Storm passing, clouds lifting
sun shining somewhat but
still persists a mist
on your countenance.

WEDNESDAY, FEBRUARY 23, 1944

A bird sings in your heart
as you watch Peter chop
and you gaze outside.
Hope sprouts wings
beholds wondrous nature
and your spirit soars with
the beauty of God's world.
His remedy being your words.
Happiness in a nutshell.

Sunday, February 27, 1944

Images of Peter
envelope you and
a strong desire to
melt the ice,
to break the barrier,
to crack the wall,
comes over you
as you long to
know him better.

MONDAY, FEBRUARY 28, 1944

Peter's carpentry
took him away.
How can one be
jealous of wood?
Creaking, knocking
noises overhead
or is it your
heart breaking?

WEDNESDAY, MARCH 1, 1944

Burglary comes to the forefront
of your minds...
opened doors,
messes made,
locks intact.
Who?
Skeleton key?
Warehouseman?
Suspicion rises
to new heights
and imagination
scales its peak.

THURSDAY, MARCH 2, 1944

Margot's miseries
confided in Mummy
are deflected like
a coat of armor.
Your own shield being
silent.
Inner opinions
sometime expressed,
sometimes not.
Blooming, growing—
not cultivated by
adults but nonetheless
there.
Always present
always challenging
as you grow and change.
A longing for respect.

FRIDAY, MARCH 3, 1944

Candle burning
and a carried torch
for Peter,
your confidante.
Eye winking
and knowing looks
convey words
that don't easily come
and in your heart
you have a deep
realization of what
a heart is truly for.
Love.

SATURDAY, MARCH 4, 1944

Taking a day trip
to seventh heaven,
you pack literature
and love.
Life has a purpose and
your purpose
has a life—
Peter.

MONDAY, MARCH 6, 1944

Quiet inwardly,
loud outwardly,
passionate within
and lonely without
his presence.

Like metal you
are drawn to
his magnet of
clumsy sweetness.

TUESDAY, MARCH 7, 1944

You view your
past as though a movie.
All the freedom,
friends and fun
play before you
like a screenplay and
you compare the
old and new Anne.
Superficial and social,
she peers back at you,
laughing.
You like her but
find her shallow,
finding life's real meaning
in love, nature and God.

SUNDAY, MARCH 12, 1944

Personal relationships
spin around you
like a web.
Spun by Margot,
Peter and
others.
Always untangling,
always unraveling
mysteries of the
connections.
Complicated and
intricate.

TUESDAY, MARCH 14, 1944

You consider everyone's moods
and the state of the pantry.
Paltry rations consist
of no fats,
rotten spuds, kale
and porridge.

Optimism and pessimism
fly side-by-side
like a twin engine jet.
Will it suck in a bird
of conflict
and crash?

WEDNESDAY, MARCH 15, 1944

Illness prevalent,
you hear of
examinations done over
the phone.
Henk tells tales
of the world outside
helping to let you
see past the
crack in the window.

THURSDAY, MARCH 16, 1944

Like a turtle in a shell,
you draw inside yourself
and the attic offers
room to examine
your true colors.
Does Peter see them,
or is he color blind?

Friday, March 17, 1944

A bird of maturity
struggles to escape
its cage.
Always peered at,
always dominated,
it flaps its wings
against the bars
and wishes to be
set free.
Free of questioning,
free of directions,
but not free of respect.

SUNDAY, MARCH 19, 1944

Trading secrets,
you and Peter
come to see how
very alike you are,
while being very different.
Complementing
each other like
peanut butter and jelly.
Your friendship
spreads smooth
over the dry toast
of everyday life
in the Annexe.

WEDNESDAY, MARCH 22, 1944

Recalling Saturday's talk
with Peter,
there are no words
to season and eat.
Your relationship
leaves a sweet
taste in your mouth
leaving you,
smiling and
breathless.

THURSDAY, MARCH 23, 1944

Peter becomes a
complimentary mirror,
reflecting your
unrecognized beauty.
Growing to understand
each other more,
you wonder
why the adults
don't see you in the
same light.
Taking you seriously
when you joke
and laughing when
you're serious...
they don't realize
how much you feel,
think and hurt.

MONDAY, MARCH 27, 1944

Smoke curling,
tea sipping, cat sleeping,
the household
surrounds the radio.
Politics stir up
the Annexe like a
spoon in a tea cup and
you would prefer to be
the cozy underneath.

TUESDAY, MARCH 28, 1944

Discord over
frequent attic visits
erupts but doesn't
diffuse the volcano
of love
bubbling inside you.
Childlike,
loving,
strong,
brave and
clumsy—
he's won your heart.

WEDNESDAY, MARCH 29, 1944

You learn of interest in
diaries will come
after the war will end
and imagine others
reading of your Jewish life
in the Annexe.
Readers
reading between the lines
getting to know you
and feel your laughter
and tears.
To feel the hunger for
food and a
more normal life.

FRIDAY, MARCH 31, 1944

Some are cold
from a lack of coal.
Sad, from a
lack of hope.
Happy, from a
lack of loneliness.
The latter being you.
With Peter and God,
how can you lose?

SATURDAY, APRIL 1, 1944

A kiss consumes
your thoughts.
The one that awaits you.
The one that must
have faith
and present itself
upon your lips
and Peter's.

MONDAY, APRIL 3, 1944

Food cycles
introduce the concept
of one food for
breakfast, lunch and dinner.
Tomatoes, tomatoes, tomatoes
or spinach, spinach, spinach.
No surprises
until vegetables
are scarce,
to your delight.
Then peas,
potatoes, dumplings
that sink or swim
like the inhabitants
in the Annexe.

TUESDAY, APRIL 4, 1944

Tears serve to
revive you and help
you see more clearly
the gem that you are.
Sparkling and glimmering
with talent in your pen,
you wish to live
forever in your work.
(You have, Anne.)

THURSDAY, APRIL 6, 1944

Many things have molded
you to the person you are.
Your love of history
makes you the philosopher.
The study of genealogy
and film stars
creates a sense of awe
toward people
you admire
and mythology
adds a little
fantasy to your life.
A well rounded
charmer, you are.

TUESDAY, APRIL 11, 1944

Feeling secure,
Peter and Mozart,
Mouschi and a
cushion,
all is cozy
as you enjoy
Peter's company.
Ruckus over a
cushion disturbs
the beauty of it,
later to be disturbed
by burglary.
Burglary frightening
and unexpected.
Unhinging you
like a door on
the ground.
Noises at the
swinging cupboard
and fear becomes a
real member of
the household.
Bathroom duties
remind you

of the inside
while you constantly
dwell on what's
outside.

Henk and Miep enter
and see a real
collage of
your lives on the
table,
jumbled still life.

The day returns
to normal.
Danger passing,
you find yourself
in Peter's arms,
again content
but questioning
the suffering
of Jews and
wonder at God's
protection.

FRIDAY, APRIL 14, 1944

It seems that only you
are able to see the best
in worst situations.
What a noble heart
you have.
A true servant to God
and rich in gratitude
for what is right
and good.
You are old beyond
your years.

FRIDAY, APRIL 14, 1944

Your love,
a secret too great to keep
but too private to share.
Your heart, too timid
to reveal
but too honest to be sly.
Your maturity,
too young for these feelings
but too old to pretend
they don't exist.

SATURDAY, APRIL 15, 1944

A bolted door
has unbolted guilt
in Peter.
Locked out,
Kraler directs his
anger towards
Peter
and fear,
as usual,
is the key.

SUNDAY, APRIL 16, 1944

Cheek stroking,
curl touching,
close sitting,
all leading up
to the kiss.
Fleeting and sweet,
given in haste
and awaited long.

TUESDAY, APRIL 18, 1944

A second kiss
springs brings forth
beauty's chance.
Flowers bloom
like your love
and hope that
liberation
will be soon.

WEDNESDAY, APRIL 19, 1944

Heaven on earth,
Peter in your arms
and nature in your soul.
Happiness
in a nutshell.

FRIDAY, APRIL 21, 1944

Princess Elizabeth has
come of age.
Who shall be her Prince?
You have yours,
of age or not.
What is age anyway?

TUESDAY, APRIL 25, 1944

Security measures
create insecurity.
Tension in Dussel pulls
like a knotted rope.
Climb this rope
for a better view
and see friction
between Pim, Dussel
and Van Daan.

THURSDAY, APRIL 27, 1944

Soaking knowledge
like a sponge,
you squeeze the excess
and it dribbles onto
pages of the diary.
So much you know
for your fourteen short years.
You have lived and loved
so many years in
just a few.

FRIDAY, APRIL 28, 1944

You shed the outer Anne
like a snakeskin
and Peter sees the
sensitive, caring Anne.
Tear streaked face,
open as pages in a book.
Seeing yourself
reflected in his eyes,
you marvel at the
beauty of this
relationship and wonder
where it will lead.

TUESDAY, MAY 2, 1944

Honesty has driven you
to reveal your fondness
for Peter to the paternal figure
and caution is ushered in
like a crisp breeze.
Watching the leaves of
advised self-control fly by,
you long to hold on to
the relationship and
weather the storm.

WEDNESDAY, MAY 3, 1944

Peter's cat Boche
has spent her ninth life—
perhaps a meal
or a fur hat.
Your pantry
has spent its best,
now its boiled lettuce
or rotten potatoes.
Your lifestyle
has spent its normalcy,
now it's confinement
and a desperation
to find humor in
dangerous situations.

FRIDAY, MAY 5, 1944

Discouraged from attic trips,
you crave trust from Pim
and closeness with Peter.
A profession of independence
displays your feelings
toward your treatment
and desire for respect
but draws silence
for the recipient.
A quiet observance of
the outside reveals
a noisy realm of murder and theft.
Will your love be
stolen away?

SUNDAY, MAY 7, 1944

Confronted by Pim,
his hurt feelings
glisten like
ice on branches.
You see past the
freeze and notice
a dripping thaw of
forgiveness.
Warmed,
you look inwardly
and see continual
looking outward
is important, too.

MONDAY, MAY 8, 1944

Grandparents, dead and gone
along with their riches.
You hear stories of a
pampered youth,
Mummy's and Daddy's.
Decent food
eaten and gone,
you eat porridge,
potatoes and spinach.
Popeye you are not
but your hopes for the
future are muscle bound.

TUESDAY, MAY 9, 1944

Your lifestyle is
threatened at 2 p.m.
by one on the outside.
A business person,
a box luncher,
someone with freedoms
will steal yours away.
No moving,
no going upstairs,
no potato delivery.
How to send
her away?

WEDNESDAY, MAY 10, 1944

Mouschi attic crouching
and finding
boxed wet dirt,
chose a spot,
christening unexpected.
Stockings,
books, a table.
Her business as usual
became yours unfortunately.
Fortunately, the
Queen will soon
push for liberation
for those in camps,
and prison and
in hiding.
A chance for normal
lives again,
as normal a life as
Jews can have.

THURSDAY, MAY 11, 1944

Subjects of your studies
encircle you,
dancing around you,
hands entwined,
you crave time to chase
each one,
fully knowing all there is to know.
This knowledge,
blooming and expanding,
bursts forth with
urges toward journalism.
A way to live
everything twice,
once through living,
twice through writing.

SATURDAY, MAY 13, 1944

Celebration.
Pim's birthday
and all seems
bright as the sun.
The day is delightful
as the pastries,
uplifting as the
flowers
and as sweet/sour
as the yogurt.

TUESDAY, MAY 16, 1944

The Van Daans
are cutting the blackberry
pie of politics.
Chewing hard
and spitting seeds
at each other.
The outcome is
crusty and angry.

FRIDAY, MAY 19, 1944

Love hungry Peter
begging for second kisses,
your heart goes out,
though wrapped in
a thin shell,
concealing the inner Anne.
Revealed before,
you reeled it back
like a fish on a line,
the hook had worked,
there was no need
to return it to the waters
of your conquest.

SATURDAY, MAY 20, 1944

Carnations lay not so lovely,
amidst vase, water, soaked books.
Your life lies wet like a
sponge on the floor as
you stand weeping
at the loss.
Sadly, you see the Algebra book
was not included in the bath.

MONDAY, MAY 22, 1944

Bets are waged over
the coming invasion
and talk of it comes
as frequently as
taking a breath.
Realization of
growing hatred
and prejudice
saddens you and
you look at Holland
as a city to which
you don't truly belong.

THURSDAY, MAY 25, 1944

Rumbling tummies
sing a song
of a discovered vegetable man.
Captured and gone,
the keeper of two Jews—
due paying is now.
Eating less
and worrying more.
You skip breakfast
and chew anxiety.

FRIDAY, MAY 26, 1944

Lives of those outside
and those inside are
as different as night and day.
Parties/misery
fancy cakes/bad food
films/fear
concerts/uncertainty.

If only for just a little while,
you could escape
this prison of two years,
this restlessness
that never ends.

WEDNESDAY, MAY 31, 1944

A butter melting,
milk souring,
sweat dripping
heat has settled.
Coloring the moods of
the inhabitants
like a huge paintbrush
filled with fiery red paint
stroked back and forth,
affecting everything
in its path.

MONDAY, JUNE 5, 1944

Butter is smooth
but arguments over it
are not.
Dussel and a Mrs.
flirt
and your life flirts
with danger—
scarce food and
fear of bombings.

Tuesday, June 6, 1944

D-Day has come
with all its promised hope
and invasion brings
thoughts of possible
return to school
in the fall.
To learn of military support
has been the best
lesson of all.

FRIDAY, JUNE 9, 1944

Despite the invasion,
your fascination with
a life history of
Franz Liszt,
composer and womanizer
has you mesmerized
by his genius and art,
repulsed by his reputation.
For you,
fair and noble
obsessed with the
finest things in life,
literature and art,
impatient with
man's shortfalls,
applaud his craft,
but not his craftiness.

TUESDAY, JUNE 13, 1944

Books, sweets and flowers,
celebrate your fifteen years.
Somehow you seem
much older
with all your insight
and your reflections
on the war.

WEDNESDAY, JUNE 14, 1944

Like a barrel of
bobbing apples,
criticism and accusations
bob up and down in
your mind—
never giving you peace.
Striving for
true happiness,
for honest soul searching
with another,
no cover-ups,
no pretense.

THURSDAY, JUNE 15, 1944

To gaze at the sun,
the moon, the stars,
a truly rich state
that would be.
Beauty taken for granted,
allowed for many,
denied for others,
awaits past the
shuttered windows
like closed eyes
in the night.

FRIDAY, JUNE 16, 1944

Mrs. Van Daan
speaks terms of desperation,
spits fire over the smoking
and feeds fuel to an
unrequited love.
Knowing how to throw water
on fire in the Annexe,
you get a bucket of laughter
to douse smoldering coals.

FRIDAY, JUNE 23, 1944

Meat and potatoes,
the meat of the news
is English are attacking
at Cherbourg,
the news of potatoes,
is there aren't many.
One potato,
two potato,
three potato,
four–
potato rationing...

TUESDAY, JUNE 27, 1944

The English
have a harbor
and you harbor
feelings of hope.

FRIDAY, JUNE 30, 1944

Three more cities
have fallen.
The tides are turning.
You want to ride
a wave in,
foam for freedom.

THURSDAY, JULY 6, 1944

A co-dependency
from Peter
brings an exam of
his backbone—
there is none.
How do you
build one?
Words like "easy"
threaten its strength
and "gamble"
threaten its
integrity.
No evidence of religion
or conscience
serve to weaken it.
In contrast, your backbone
serves as a grand
example.

SATURDAY, JULY 8, 1944

Up to your necks in
strawberries
at every turn.
Stewed, sugared,
jammed, jellied.
Supply exceeds demand
but you must eat.
Then it's peas,
green and menacing,
tasty torture of
strings and pods
and boring work.

SATURDAY, JULY 15, 1944

An uncanny ability,
you examine yourself,
as though detached,
you see courage,
justice and
idealism.
Empathy affords suffering
for those in need
and a loving heart
searching out
the good in people.

FRIDAY, JULY 21, 1944

An attempt on Hitler's life
gives you more hope
for yours.
With your mind's eye,
in the far distance,
you can see school
waiting there
with all its riches of
knowledge.
So close and yet
so far away.

TUESDAY, AUGUST 1, 1944

"Contradictory"
you've been dubbed.
Like a budding tree,
its roots come from
a deeply embedded
split personality.
The quick, witty Anne and
the slow, solemn Anne.
The latter being
hidden from view,
shown only to you.
If only you could
be your true self
to the world.
If only you could
let them know the
whole beautiful you.

EPILOGUE—
FRIDAY, AUGUST 4, 1944

The raid on the Annexe
that was no longer
secret, toppled
your security and home.
Concentration camps
were the fate of
all and Pim returned alone.
Like part of your soul,
your diary became an
immortal
mark on your world.
Even after your
death in March 1945
at Bergen-Belsen,
Anne, you are
with us still...

Phyllis Johnson's unique way with words has been featured in many popular newspapers and magazines, including:

Woman's World
Working Mother
Tidewater Parent
Designed to Flourish
Virginia Teacher
Tidewater Teacher
Country Woman
Contempo
The Sun
The Religious Herald
Hampton Roads Woman
The Virginian-Pilot
The Daily Press
Our Western World's Most Beautiful Poetry

In this re-released book, Phyllis Johnson reveals a pensive, empathetic mode of writing. Being Frank with Anne is sure to bring readers to further inspect the feelings and emotions found in the words and between the lines of Anne Frank's diary, a book that has both inspired and haunted Phyllis since childhood.

Phyllis lives with her husband and a black lab in Virginia, living life to its fullest and actively promoting her books through her many affiliations and media contacts. One of her latest books is a young adult suspense novel titled, inkBLOT, co-written with Nancy Naigle under the pen name, Johnson Naigle.

Read more about Phyllis C. Johnson at
www.phyllisjohnson.net

More Reviews

"Phyllis Johnson has penned a unique, insightful, and deeply reflective work of art. Her exceptionally innovative poems use familiar language to uncover profound themes lurking behind one of the most famous pieces of literature in history. This wonderfully original and startlingly insightful approach rapidly reveals the heart-breaking humanity behind Anne Frank's original words, bringing us closer to her as living person – her hopes, her fears, and her dreams Instantly readable and utterly engrossing, this book creates images that will linger in the mind of the reader long after the final page has been turned."

- Dr. Rich Allen, Educational Psychologist

"Johnson's poetic insights into Anne Frank's incredible and heart-wrenching experience make for powerful reading. For those who have read the diary, this will deepen understanding. Those who read Being Frank with Anne first will want to share it with someone and then locate a copy of the diary. Students are bound to find this small but captivating volume a great companion to their classroom study of the diary. Teachers will want to incorporate this book into their lessons and everyone who reads it will experience the sights, sounds, and smells within that hidden place that has become part of the world's conscience."

- Ron Nash

"Powerfully moving poetry"

- Prof. Bill Ruehlmann, Virginia Wesleyan College

"Phyllis has presented another approach to the Anne Frank story. A unique and memorable experience."

- Mark Weston, playwright of *Harry and Eddie, the Birth of Israel* starring Ed Asner

11032581R00117

Made in the USA
Charleston, SC
25 January 2012